D1203081

Fabulous FASHIONs of the 1970s

Felicia Lowenstein
NIVEN

Fabulous FASHIONs of the DECADES

Enslow Publishers, Inc.
40 Industrial Road
Box 398
Berkeley Heights, NJ 07922
USA

http://www.enslow.com

Library of Congress Cataloging-in-Publication Data
Niven, Felicia Lowenstein.
    Fabulous fashions of the 1970s / Felicia Lowenstein Niven.
       p. cm. — (Fabulous fashions of the decades)
    Fabulous fashions of the nineteen seventies
    Includes bibliographical references and index.
    Summary: "Discusses the fashions of the 1970s, including women's and men's clothing and hair-
      styles, accessories, trends and fads, and world events that influenced the fashion"—Provided by
      publisher.
    ISBN 978-0-7660-3826-4
    1. Fashion—History—20th century—Juvenile literature. 2. Fashion design—History—20th
      century—Juvenile literature. 3. Lifestyle—History—20th century—Juvenile literature.
    4. Nineteen seventies—Juvenile literature. I. Title. II. Title: Fabulous fashions of the nineteen
      seventies.
    TT504.N5815 2011
    746.9'2—dc22

2010014589

Paperback ISBN: 978-1-59845-280-8

Printed in the United States of America

052011 Lake Book Manufacturing, Inc., Melrose Park, IL

10 9 8 7 6 5 4 3 2 1

To Our Readers: We have done our best to make sure all Internet Addresses in this book were active and appropriate when we went to press. However, the author and the publisher have no control over and assume no liability for the material available on those Internet sites or on other Web sites they may link to. Any comments or suggestions can be sent by e-mail to comments@enslow.com or to the address on the back cover.

Every effort has been made to locate all copyright holders of material used in this book. If any errors or omissions have occurred, corrections will be made in future editions of this book.

♻ Enslow Publishers, Inc., is committed to printing our books on recycled paper. The paper in every book contains 10% to 30% post-consumer waste (PCW). The cover board on the outside of each book contains 100% PCW. Our goal is to do our part to help young people and the environment too!

Illustration Credits: Advertising Archive/courtesty Everett Collection, pp. 23, 28, 31; AP Images, p. 40; AP Images/Jeff Robbins, p. 12; AP Images/NBCU Photo Bank, p. 1; © ClassicStock/Alamy, pp. 6, 21; courtesy Everett Collection, pp. 4, 13, 33; CSU Archives/Everett Collection, p. 7; H. Armstrong Roberts/ClassicStock/Everett Collection, p. 19; Library of Congress, pp. 42–44; PA Photos/Landov, p. 17; Photo by Ray Stevenson/Rex USA, courtesy Everett Collection, p. 34; Photo by Richard Young/Rex USA, courtesy Everett Collection, p. 11; Shutterstock, pp. 5, 9, 15, 20, 25, 26, 27, 30, 36, 38, 46.

Cover Illustration: AP Images/NBCU Photo Bank (woman in short, yellow dress).

Contents

The 1970s

The 1970s

Women who had naturally straight hair, like Maureen McCormick who played Marcia Brady on *The Brady Bunch* television show, didn't have to worry about ironing their hair to be in style!

Wild and Crazy Fads

An iron sure comes in handy for keeping your clothes looking neat. In the 1970s, it had another use. Women used to iron their hair straight. Back then, there were no straightening irons, but women had a choice: they could spend a lot of money and get straight hair in a salon, or they could straighten their hair at home with an iron. It seemed dangerous, but many women did it. The woman would lay her hair on the ironing board. A friend or family member would iron her hair bit by bit very carefully. An iron that was too hot could damage the hair. It also could burn the woman or the person ironing! Today's straightening irons take much of the danger out of this crazy process!

Straight hair may have been in style for women, but curly hair was in style for men. Some men went to beauty salons for perms. That may sound odd, but men's fashion had already gotten more like women's fashion; now men's hair did, too.

Men began to wear jewelry, too. Gold chains were popular and so were peace-sign necklaces. Cool watches lit up; some could even play music! Most of men's jewelry during this time was unisex. It could be worn by a man or a woman.

As it turned out, so could men's clothes. The movie *Annie Hall* showed a woman in a man's suit. The oversized man's jacket and pants created a tomboyish look for the lead actress, Diane Keaton. The style caught on; many women copied it by taking men's clothes and making them their own.

After all, the seventies were all about individuals. In fact, it was even nicknamed the "me" decade.

A young man dressed in typical seventies clothing accented by a necklace

Introduction: Wild and Crazy Fads

People were into individual successes. They pursued individual happiness. So women could dress like men. Or they could dress like women.

Some women liked to show off their femininity, and legs, with another fashion choice—hot pants. Hot pants were really short shorts. The style was similar to silky underwear

Hot pants look flirty and fun with a pair of lace-up sandals!

in the 1920s. They were known as tap pants. In the 1970s, they were made for regular street wear. Hot pants were made from materials such as velvet, cotton, nylon, and denim. They came in solid colors and patterns.

Hot pants were a style that did not last. But other styles from the seventies did. Read on to find out more.

Chapter 1

Hairstyles

fter years of fussing with hair, it was time to look natural. The seventies hairstyles were simple and did not require a lot of work. There was no more teasing hair to the highest heights or sleeping in curlers to get that extra volume. People could literally let their hair down.

Straight hair was one of the most popular styles. It was easy for people with naturally straight hair. They could wear their hair parted down the middle and long. If they didn't have straight hair, but they wanted it, they could get it straightened in a salon; or they could try the iron trick in the previous pages. (**Note:** Do not try that at home!)

People with tightly curled hair could wear an Afro. This style created a puff of hair around the head and was very easy to maintain. Afros were worn by men and women in the seventies.

Mullets were another popular hairstyle. The cut was short in the front and long in the back. Although more popular with men, mullets were worn by women. If you didn't like the mullet, you might like the shag. This heavily layered haircut created a shaggy or slightly messy look. Looking for a cleaner look? Try the wedge cut. This short hairstyle was worn by women, including figure skater Dorothy Hamill.

Men also wore a style that hadn't been seen in years. They wore sideburns and beards. This became a very fashionable look.

In the 1970s, handheld blow-dryers were common. Men and women owned and used them. That gave way to many blow-dried styles, such as the "feathered" cut, which was a layered look that resembled feathers.

Farrah Fawcett's Feathers

Farrah Fawcett was a familiar face in the 1970s. She was as well-known for her hair as she was for her TV shows. She made the feathered look famous. This hairstyle was also known as the flip. Her long blond hair was layered along the sides. A blow-dryer was used to curve it back. The look was natural. It looked a little bit like feathers along the sides. Everyone wanted to have the Farrah cut. Both men and women wore feathered bangs and cuts.

Hairstyles

Farrah Fawcett (1947–2009) became a fashion icon when her bouncy blond tresses first appeared on the television show *Charlie's Angels* in 1976.

Dorothy Hamill's Wedge

When figure skater Dorothy Hamill won the Olympic Gold Medal in 1976, the world took note of her hair. It was short like a bowl cut, but there was a strong angle to it. It caused the hair to really move when she twirled around. Women copied the look and the wedge cut became very popular. You could wear it whether you were young or old. You just could not wear it if your hair was curly.

Dorothy Hamill's wedge cut was a good choice for women who didn't want to fuss with long hair.

Hairstyles

The Afro

If you had curly hair or if you were African-American, you could wear an Afro. Also called a "natural," an Afro was a short to medium cut. It allowed curly and African-American hair to puff out naturally. You just needed a trim to keep it in line.

The Afro gave African-American women a lot of freedom. They no longer had to sit for hours at home or at the salon with harsh chemicals on their scalps. That saved them money and time. They could also go swimming or get caught in the rain, and it would not ruin their hairstyle.

American actress Pam Grier sports a funky Afro in 1974.

The Shag

Cut short layers of hair at the top and the bottom and you have the shag haircut. Men and women wore it, sometimes with bangs. A shag could make flat hair look full if you blow-dried it, and plenty of people liked that effect. Shags were worn by many celebrities in the seventies, and they continue to be popular today.

Chapter 2

Women's Styles and Fashion

"There are no rules in fashion anymore," announced *Vogue* magazine in the 1970s. It appeared that everyone was doing his or her own thing. After all, it was the seventies and individuality ruled. The best part was that you could choose your own style and change it whenever you wanted.

Let's start at the top—with the tops. There were shirts that covered the body and those that revealed plenty of skin. Some tops were billowy and loose and others were tight-fitting. On the bottom, there were long skirts and short skirts and some in between. You could find almost anything to suit your taste.

The wraparound dress was first introduced in the 1970s. Women could just step into it like a jacket. Then they could tie it as tightly or loosely as they wanted. Designer jeans also made their debut. Tight and formfitting, they could be dressed up as easily as they could be dressed down.

There may not have been any definite fashion rules in the seventies, but there were plenty of choices!

Wrap It Around

Designer Diane von Furstenberg had seen dancers' sweaters that wrapped around. That gave her an idea for a wraparound shirt. She designed it in soft cotton jersey. It was a great idea that got even better when she made it longer. The shirt became a dress and women loved it. It was a style that looked good on everybody. That was because when you wrapped it around your body and tied it together, it hugged the figure in all the right places.

Mini, Midi, and Maxi

What length would you like your skirt? You had several choices in the seventies. The miniskirt of the sixties was still around. There was even a shorter version, called the micromini. Then you had the maxiskirt that came down to your ankles. Some people say it was a response to the miniskirt. But it was fun to have so many choices. You also had a style in between known as the midi, which covered up

Long, billowy dresses were as fashionable in the seventies as mini-skirts and hot pants.

to your knee. It was not a straight skirt in the seventies; the midi skirt or dress usually flared out a little.

All of these skirts came in a range of materials. They could be made from cotton, corduroy, polyester, denim, or velvet. They also came in plenty of colors and patterns.

Top It Off

If you liked to show off your skin, there were plenty of choices in the seventies. There were tops without sleeves, tops without bottoms, and tops without backs. Crop tops were tops that had the lower part cut off. They showed your belly. Halter tops had no backs. The straps came around your neck to hold the top up. The strapless tube top was a single band of fabric that went around your body and was held up by elastic.

Jeans by Design

Something happened to jeans during the seventies. The original boxy look became tighter and fancier. Gloria Vanderbilt, Jordache, and Calvin Klein were just some of the jean designers. They took jeans and made them formfitting. They stitched fancy designs on pockets and added big labels.

They added even more to the price tag. Designer jeans cost about twice what regular jeans cost. The makers spent a lot of money on advertising. But it must have convinced women because they ignored the high prices and bought them anyway!

The designer jeans fit so tightly that women sometimes had to lie down on the floor to squeeze into them. They would have to inhale before they zipped them up. Now that was a dedication to fashion!

Jeans were no longer just for casual affairs. You could dress them up or down and they came in many styles, from hip-hugging, skinny jeans to high-waisted, wide-legged jeans, like in the photograph here.

Chapter 3

Men's Styles and Fashion

Men and women shared some styles in the 1970s. They both wore platform shoes and bell-bottom pants. They wore colorful caftans, flowing tops from the Far East.

But there were some fashions that were just for men. Three-piece suits were in style. These included a matching vest as well as pants and a jacket. But in the 1970s, the suits were not in dark or boring colors. They were white, pastel, and brightly colored, too. Some even had patterns, such as plaid.

For everyday wear, men wore leisure suits. These were matching tops and bottoms that were named for relaxation, or leisure. Leisure suits were dressier than jogging suits.

Of course, men wore those, too, mostly to exercise. However, some people wore jogging suits to make fashion statements as well.

Flannel and gauze shirts were in every man's closet. Jeans continued to be a wardrobe staple and fit right in with the popular cowboy look of the seventies. To achieve this look, men would tuck their jeans into boots and wear rawhide belts with patterns. They also wore Western shirts, which were long-sleeved button-downs with fancy designs, and, of course, cowboy hats!

If that sounds familiar, it probably is. Many of these styles are still with us today.

This man is all business in a pastel plaid suit.

Not Too Cheesy!

Designers made clothes out of all sorts of materials. One such cloth was cheesecloth. It was a loosely woven cotton that was a little like gauze. Originally the material was used to press cheese. But the fabric was ideal for clothing. It was strong, great for hot weather, and did not need ironing. Cheesecloth shirts came in many colors and styles. They were a common sight in the seventies.

The New Play Suit

Many men said "good-bye" to the business suit and "hello" to the leisure suit. These new suits were casual and comfortable. They had jackets that looked like shirts. They had matching pants. Both were made out of stretchable polyester. Men wore them at work, on dates, shopping, or even playing golf.

Sportswear

Sports stars began to endorse products. Designer logos were on their sneakers and clothes. You started to see the Converse star and the Nike wave. They started to appear on the sportswear that ordinary men could buy.

Jogging suits became very popular, especially as running and exercise became more commonplace. The suits were fashion statements in and of themselves. They came in different colors, often with matching headbands.

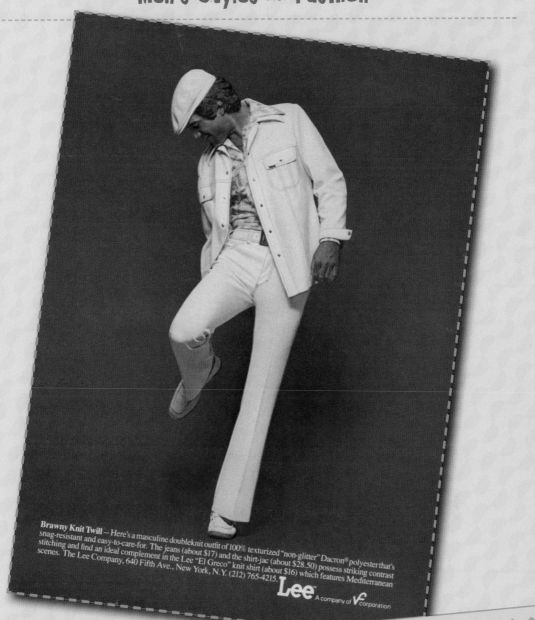

Brawny Knit Twill — Here's a masculine doubleknit outfit of 100% texturized "non-glitter" Dacron® polyester that's snag-resistant and easy-to-care-for. The jeans (about $17) and the shirt-jac (about $28.50) possess striking contrast stitching and find an ideal complement in the Lee "El Greco" knit shirt (about $16) which features Mediterranean scenes. The Lee Company, 640 Fifth Ave., New York, N.Y. (212) 765-4215.

Lee A company of ƒ corporation

Men didn't have to choose between style and comfort. A leisure suit provided both!

Men wore them to exercise, but they also wore them for casual wear. It would not be unusual to see a jogging suit at a party or at a disco.

Crazy for Caftans

Men often wore clothing from other countries. These clothes had simple shapes and interesting details. For example, they might have embroidery or an exotic print. Men wore loose-fitting shirts called caftans and hooded cloaks called djellabas. Designers were inspired by fashions from places like Morocco, India, and Japan. They created clothes that had many of those details.

4

Accessories

Many accessories were shared by both women and men. For example, women had been wearing platform shoes for a few decades now. They became big in the seventies, and even men's shoemakers took the plunge.

Men and women also wore some of the same jewelry. Puka shell chokers were popular. So were mood rings and necklaces. Those changed color depending on your mood.

Handmade was also in style and there was a great interest in crafts. It was a part of the individual expression of the seventies. People experimented with textiles. They made macramé bags and plant hangers. Many teens did their knot tying when making friendship bracelets. With a little time and concentration, you could have a nice accessory—and a meaningful present for your friend.

Plenty of Puka

Actor and singer David Cassidy went to Hawaii on vacation. He brought back a souvenir, a necklace made from puka shells. He wore it on his TV show, *The Partridge Family*. Other teen idols started wearing the style. That started a national craze.

Everyone wanted a puka shell necklace. *Puka* means "hole" in Hawaiian. The necklaces were made from the tiny, white shells of cone snails found in Hawaii. The shells had natural holes where you could thread the string. You could buy real or fake puka shell chokers.

In the Mood

How are you feeling? If you had a mood ring, it could tell you. The mood ring was invented by Joshua Reynolds. He took a heat-sensitive liquid crystal and put it inside quartz, a clear hard material. The crystal would change color depending on your body temperature. Mood rings came with a color guide. Blue meant happy. Purple meant moody. Black meant depressed. Yellow meant tense.

Whoever wore this ring wasn't in such a good mood!

The mood ring and necklace turned out to be big fads in the seventies. They did not always choose the right mood, but they were fun to talk about!

F Is for Friendship Bracelet

The rule was simple. Friendship bracelets were worn until they fell off. Cutting it off meant the friendship had ended. These bracelets were worn by both men and women. They were handmade, tying knots on some sort of string or yarn. Some people made designs such as candy stripes or totem poles and added colored beads.

You could buy these woven bracelets at a store, but it was more fun and more meaningful to give and receive homemade ones!

A Step Up

Get ready to add a few inches to your height. Step into the platform shoes of the seventies. Both men and women wore platforms. This footwear had a sole and heel that were several inches thick. It was like you were walking on a platform. The thick soles were made from many materials.

The most popular may have been cork because it was so lightweight. But platforms also came in plastic, rubber, and wood. There were platform shoes, boots, and sandals. There were even platform sneakers!

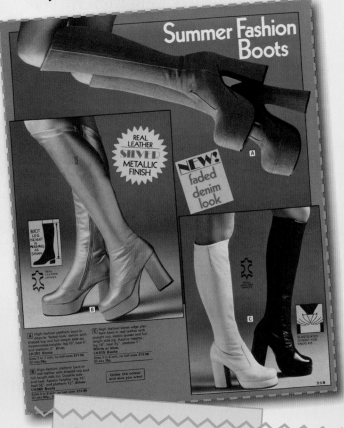

Platform shoes, especially boots like these, are still worn today!

Down to Earth

Danish yoga instructor Anne Kalso had an idea about posture. She thought that if you put your heel below your toes, it would be easier to stand up straight. That was the idea behind her invention, the Earth shoe. This ultracomfortable shoe had a heel that was thinner than the sole.

Earth shoes were so popular in the seventies that if you didn't own a pair, you probably knew several people who did. They only came in one basic brown style back then. Today they are available in many colors and styles.

Chapter 5
Fads and Trends

What was your style? In the seventies, you could be a disco queen or king. You could be a punk rocker. You could have an old-fashioned look. These were all popular trends.

Disco was very widespread. It was especially popular among young people. They used to gather at clubs each weekend to dance. Disco clothes made it easy to dance. They allowed the body to move to the disco beat.

Punk-rock music was very different. It paired powerful words with a fast-paced rhythm that was not as easy for dancing. The message of the songs spoke out against society. It is no wonder that punk style was designed to be antifashion.

The opposite of punk was the old-fashioned look. People looked like they stepped back in time. They dressed like they did in the 1800s.

But no matter what look you chose, chances are that you didn't give up your jeans. By now, everyone had a pair of denim jeans in his or her closet. But that was not the end of what you could do with denim. In the seventies, denim was used for much more.

Denim, Denim, and More Denim

People wore denim jackets. They wore jean skirts, both mini and maxi. Some designers simply took old denim and made it into new. They opened the inseam and added pieces of material to the front and back.

The All-Together Separate-Lees — From the people who brought you the Leesure Suit comes the Separate Lees Suit.™ a tastefully tailored ensemble composed of jacket (about $40), vest and jeans (each about $18). All Lee-Set™ 100% cotton to resist wrinkling, shrinking and puckering. And all designed to subtly inter-change with Separate-Lees to create looks to suit the occasion or your mood. The added touch: A Lee "Sub..." $16). The Lee Company, 640 Fifth Avenue, New York 10019. (212) 765-4215. ■ A Lee "Sub...

The three-piece denim suit was an interesting twist on both jeans and suits!

People also enjoyed new colors of denim. The traditional blue of course was popular. But you could get denim in beige, pink, and tan. Some denim had patterns such as checks or flowers woven through it. People also added patches of bright patterned fabrics to jeans as decoration.

There was even denim that was not denim. The material was copied onto other fabrics such as polyester.

Disco Fever

Going to a discotheque? You can't just wear anything. In fact, disco dance wear was very distinct for both women and men.

Women wore leotards with tights and wraparound skirts. For fashion's sake, at least two of the three would be in different colors. There were all sorts of women's outfits designed specifically for disco dancing. Some had rhinestones, sequins, or glitter. They looked a little like skating outfits. Most importantly, they were stretchy and pliable and easy to dance in.

Men wore tight-fitting pants and silky shirts in bright colors or patterns. They also sometimes dressed up like John Travolta in the 1977 hit movie *Saturday Night Fever*. Travolta played a young man in a dead-end job who was king of the disco on Saturday night. His famous disco look in the movie was a white three-piece suit with a black shirt.

Where do you go when the record is over...

Many men copied John Travolta's look from *Saturday Night Fever.*

The Peasant Look

The peasant look was also part of seventies fashion. Designers like Laura Ashley drew on styles and details from Victorian times and the clothes worn by early American settlers. She created blouses with high-necked ruffles and long skirts that reached the ankle. Sometimes the skirts were edged with ruffles or lace.

The dresses were often made in cotton printed with tiny patterns. One popular pattern was paisley. This was a tear-shaped floral design, popular in Scotland. Worn with lace-up "granny" boots, the style was a modern take on an old-fashioned look.

The Nonstyle: Punk

Dressing "punk" drew much attention. This style came out in the seventies. It was connected to punk-rock music. It was a sort of antifashion. In other words, punk rockers tried not to be fashionable. They dyed their hair strange colors, such as green, pink, or orange. They then styled their hair with gel to shape it. Both men and women also wore dark eye makeup.

Punk clothes might include torn jeans, leather jackets, school blazers, animal print pants, plaid, and items with lots of zippers. Punk accessories included dog collars worn by people. Safety pins and chains were part of the look, too. Many people still dress in punk style today.

The British punk-rock band Siouxsie (pronounced like the name Suzie) and the Banshees perform in 1977. Punk rockers may wear dramatic makeup and spiky hair to express themselves.

Chapter 6
Pop Culture

It was an interesting time in the United States. The Women's Liberation Movement was underway. Liberation means "freedom."

Not all women were "women's libbers." But the ones that were part of the movement joined together to protest sexist social injustices. They wanted equal pay for a job done by a man or a woman. They wanted more decision-making women in government. They wanted women to have opportunities in business and education. In short, women wanted to be treated the same way as men.

Women's Lib was perfect for the seventies. After all, it was known as the "me" decade. People became fascinated with themselves; they focused on their own happiness. They concentrated on what was important to them. They also enjoyed their leisure time, and there was plenty to do.

Disco was the hot new music, and it was made for dancing. Women and men joined together on the dance floor. With disco, you could do line dances. You could dance with one another.

People also started moving their bodies outside the clubs. Fashion and sports came together as being fit came into style. Exercise videos were popular; so were the clothes. Exercise was a craze that was here to stay.

Another type of craze was really silly. But the seventies seemed like the perfect time for it. People started collecting pet rocks. After all, they were clean, cheap, and well-behaved pets.

Pet Rocks—Yes, Rocks!

Everyone wants a pet that is fun to play with and easy to care for. That was the idea behind Pet Rocks, invented by California ad executive Gary Dahl in 1975. He thought people would have fun with the ideal pet. It was not messy. It did not need food. It came in lots of shapes and colors.

Dahl thought he could sell his idea. He made it as much like a real pet as possible. He wrote a Pet Rock Training Manual. He put the rocks in a cardboard pet carrier with some straw at the bottom. They were a big hit when they first came out, but the Pet Rock fad quickly faded away by the following year.

Disco Dancing

The disco sound was big and the beat was fast. Millions of young people came out to the clubs to dance to it. Line dances like the Hustle were popular. People could dance together as a group or with each other as a couple.

Donna Summer and the BeeGees were popular disco artists. The BeeGees recorded the soundtrack for the 1977 disco movie *Saturday Night Fever* starring John Travolta. He spent his days working at a job he did not like. But he spent his nights as king of the disco. *Saturday Night Fever* helped disco become even more popular.

Mirror balls were used in dance clubs long before disco music came onto the scene, but they have since become symbolic of the disco era. When light hits the spinning ball, each tiny mirror reflects a beam of light, creating a swirling polka-dot effect in the room.

Workout Time

It may seem normal to see people exercise. But until the seventies, there was not a lot of it. You got exercise if you worked a job that made you sweat or from doing housework. But you did not "work out."

That changed in the seventies. People had free time, and they used it to exercise. They rode exercise bikes, ran, swam, and did yoga. Health became big business as clubs opened with swimming pools and exercise rooms. There were special fitness clothes, too. It was a trend that would be with us for a long time.

The Women's Movement

Women had come a long way since they first fought for the right to vote in 1920. But there was still a need for a Women's Rights Movement. Women may have had jobs, but they were not getting equal pay for equal work. They also were not able to work everywhere that men worked. They did not always have the same opportunities for advancement.

The Women's Liberation Movement fought for women. Groups like the National Organization for Women (NOW) and the Women's Equity Action League (WEAL) helped to get the word out. There were protests and marches. Women wrote about the challenges.

Women demonstrate around the statue of American Civil War navy officer Admiral David G. Farragut in Washington, D.C., in 1970. Their signs urge women to stand together against gender discrimination.

Some in the Women's Movement said that women were slaves to fashion. They did not want women to dress to please society or men. They wanted them to dress for themselves.

Today's feminists, or those who fight for women's rights and interests, have changed that view. They have been able to embrace both fashion and equal rights.

Timeline

The 1920s

The look: cloche hats, dropped-waist dresses, long strands of pearls (women), and baggy pants (men)

The hair: short bobs

The fad: raccoon coats

The 1930s

The look: dropped hemlines, natural waists, practical shoes (women), and blazers and trousers (men)

The hair: finger waves and permanents

The fad: sunbathing

The 1940s

The look: shirtwaist dresses and military style (women) and suits and fedoras (men)

The hair: victory rolls and updos

The fad: kangaroo cloaks

The 1950s

The look: circular skirts and saddle shoes (women) and the greaser look (men)

The hair: bouffants and pompadours

The fad: coonskin caps

The 1960s

The look: bell-bottoms and miniskirts (women) and turtlenecks and hipster pants (men)

The hair: beehives and pageboys

The fad: go-go boots

The 1970s

The look: designer jeans (women) and leisure suits (men)

The hair: shags and Afros

The fad: hot pants

The 1980s

The look: preppy (women and men) and *Miami Vice* (men)

The hair: side ponytails and mullets

The fad: ripped off-the-shoulder sweatshirts

The 1990s

The look: low-rise, straight-leg jeans (both women and men)

The hair: the "Rachel" cut from *Friends*

The fad: ripped, acid-washed jeans

The 2000s

The look: leggings and long tunic tops (women) and the sophisticated urban look (men)

The hair: feminine, face-framing cuts (with straight hair dominating over curly)

The fad: organic and bamboo clothing

Glossary

accessories—Items that are not part of your main clothing but worn with it, for example, jewelry, gloves, hats, and belts.

Afro—A short to medium haircut that puffs around the head, usually worn by people with really curly hair.

crop top— A shirt cut off at the midriff.

disco—Fast-paced dance music popular in the 1970s.

fad—A short-term craze.

fashion—The current style of dressing.

flannel—A cotton fabric.

flared—Wider at the bottom edge.

gauze—A thin, transparent fabric.

halter top— A backless shirt with a strap that comes around the neck to hold it up.

leisure—Free time.

maxiskirt—An ankle-length skirt.

midi (skirt)—A knee-length skirt.

miniskirt— A short skirt that ends above the knee.

mullet— A haircut that is short in the front and long in the back.

puka shell—The tiny, white shell of the Hawaiian cone snail, often used to make necklaces.

shag—A layered haircut.

tomboy—A girl that dresses or acts like a boy.

trend—The current style or general direction for fashion.

tube top—A strapless shirt made out of a single band of fabric that wraps around the torso.

wedge—An angled bowl haircut for women.

Further Reading

Books

Beker, Jeanne. *Passion for Fashion: Careers in Style.* Toronto, Canada: Tundra Books, 2008.

Harris, Nathaniel. *The 1970s.* Mankato, Minn.: Arcturus Publishing, 2010.

Herald, Jacqueline. *Fashions of a Decade: The 1970s.* New York: Facts On File, 2006.

Jones, Jen. *Fashion History: Looking Great Through the Ages.* Mankato, Minn.: Capstone Press, 2007.

Internet Addresses

Fashion-Era, "The 70s Disco Fashion"
<http://www.fashion-era.com/1970s.htm>

70s Fashion
<http://www.70sfashion.org/>

Index

47